BASKETBALL'S
—GREATEST—
NICKNAMES

Chocolate Thunder, Spoon, The Brow, and More!

by

THOM STORDEN

CAPSTONE PRESS
a capstone imprint

Capstone Captivate is published by Capstone Press, an imprint of Capstone.
1710 Roe Crest Drive
North Mankato, Minnesota 56003
capstonepub.com

SPORTS ILLUSTRATED KIDS is a trademark of ABG-SI LLC. Used with permission.

Library of Congress Cataloging-in-Publication Data is available on the Library of Congress website.
ISBN: 9781663906878 (hardcover)
ISBN: 9781663920416 (paperback)
ISBN: 9781663906847 (ebook pdf)

Summary: Many of the greatest basketball players have earned funny, odd, or interesting nicknames during their careers. Read to find out the stories behind basketball's legendary nicknames.

Image Credits
Alamy: Emanuel Tanjala, 25; Associated Press: Jeff Chiu, 12, Nick Wass, 22, Sue Ogrocki, 5, Susan Ragan, 27; Getty Images: Bettmann, 14; Newscom: Brian Rothmuller/Icon Sportswire, 9, SportsChrome, 4; Shutterstock: Alter-ego, (ball) Cover, Tiwat K, (doodle) Cover; Sports Illustrated: Erick W. Rasco, 26, 28, John Biever, 20, John D. Hanlon, 8, John W. McDonough, 19, Manny Millan, 6, 10, 21, 23, 29, Robert Beck, 16

Editorial Credits
Editor: Erika L. Shores; Designer: Terri Poburka; Media Researcher: Morgan Walters; Production Specialist: Laura Manthe

All internet sites appearing in back matter were available and accurate when this book was sent to press.

All records and statistics in this book are current through the 2020 season.

Printed and bound in the United States of America. PO4270

TABLE OF CONTENTS

Words in **BOLD** are in the glossary.

Nicknames of the Hardwood

In 1891, Dr. James Naismith invented the game of basketball. Soon after, some players started collecting nicknames. For each outstanding dribble, pass, 3-pointer, or dunk, there's a player who made their mark.

One of the first greats of the game was George Mikan. He was called Mr. Basketball. Later, Wilt "The Stilt" Chamberlain and Oscar "The Big O" Robertson broke **records**. No one will forget Earvin "Magic" Johnson or Michael "Air" Jordan in the 1980s and 1990s. And today, James "The Beard" Harden and Anthony "The Brow" Davis rule the court.

Anthony "The Brow" Davis is one of many standout NBA players with a nickname.

Wilt "The Stilt" Chamberlain played for the Los Angeles Lakers from 1968 to 1973.

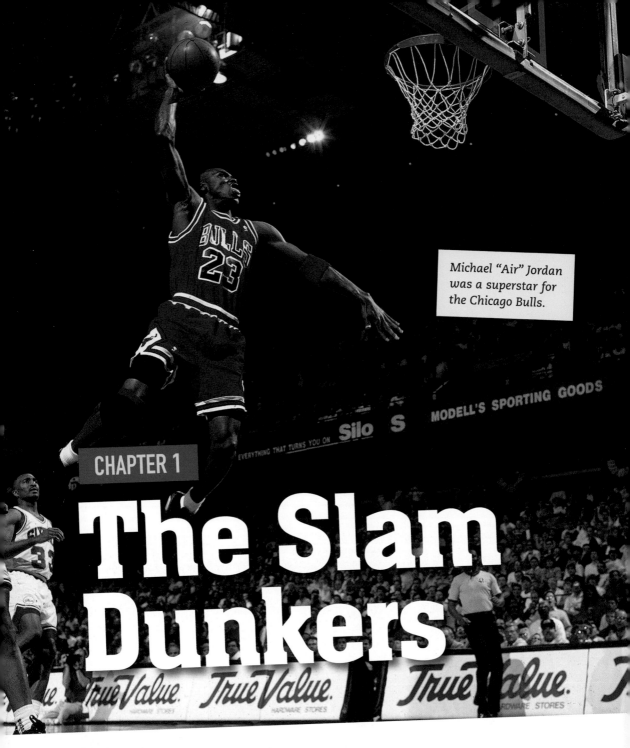

Michael "Air" Jordan was a superstar for the Chicago Bulls.

CHAPTER 1

The Slam Dunkers

The slam dunk is a nickname itself. At first it was called a "stuff shot." Later on, Chick Hearn, a **sportscaster** for the Los Angeles Lakers, began calling it a "slam dunk." Many fans think it's the game's most exciting play.

DARRYL DAWKINS:
Chocolate Thunder

Darryl Dawkins was the first player to turn pro right after high school. He became a star center for the Philadelphia 76ers. Dawkins dunked hard. His dunks broke glass backboards twice in 1979.

Dawkins nicknamed his best power dunks. He called one of his glass-breakers the Chocolate-Thunder-Flyin'-Babies-Cryin'-Rump-Roastin'-Bun-Toastin'-Thank-You-M'am-Wham-Bam-I-Am-Jam.

MICHAEL "Air" JORDAN

Many people say Michael Jordan was the greatest basketball player of all time. Jordan had the perfect dunking nickname—Air. When Jordan jumped, it seemed like he could float forever.

AIR-INSPIRED

Many players earned spin-off nicknames for their likeness to Michael Jordan. Harold Miner had a shaved head like Jordan. Miner was nicknamed Baby Jordan. Vince Carter played for the Toronto Raptors. He went to the University of North Carolina like Jordan. He was nicknamed Air Canada. Andrew Wiggins, who grew up in Canada, was called Maple Jordan. Dunk master Aaron Gordon became Air Gordon. He has shown off his soaring leaps in NBA Slam Dunk Contests.

JULIUS "**Dr. J**" ERVING

Dr. J was known for his graceful slam dunks. He got his name from a childhood friend. This friend called him The Doctor because Erving called him The Professor. In the pros Dr. J would float through the air to make a "house call." Crowds cheered his swooping dunks.

DOMINIQUE WILKINS:
The Human Highlight Film

Watching video of Dominique Wilkins's rim attacks, fans can see where he got his nickname. The Human Highlight Film starred for the Atlanta Hawks from 1982 to 1994. He was the NBA Slam Dunk Contest champ in 1985 and 1990.

Dr. J's first pro team was the Virginia Squires in the 1971–72 season.

Donovan Mitchell won the NBA dunk contest in 2018.

DONOVAN MITCHELL:
Spida

A former teammate's dad gave Donovan Mitchell his nickname. He thought Mitchell's long arms and speed were spiderlike. On top of that, Mitchell was a fan of the superhero Spider-Man as a kid. Spida won the NBA Slam Dunk Contest in 2018.

DAVID "Skywalker" THOMPSON

Skywalker rose to fame as a college player. During his college years, dunking was against the rules. But Skywalker slammed it plenty in the pros, where it was allowed. The Denver Nuggets star had an amazing 44-inch (112-centimeter) vertical leap. It made him look like he could walk on air.

BEST OF THE REST: More Great Dunker Nicknames

Darrell Griffith: **Dr. Dunkenstein**

Vince Carter: **Vinsanity**

Clyde **"The Glide"** Drexler

Hakeem **"The Dream"** Olajuwon

Rik Smits: **The Dunking Dutchman**

Kenny **"Sky"** Walker

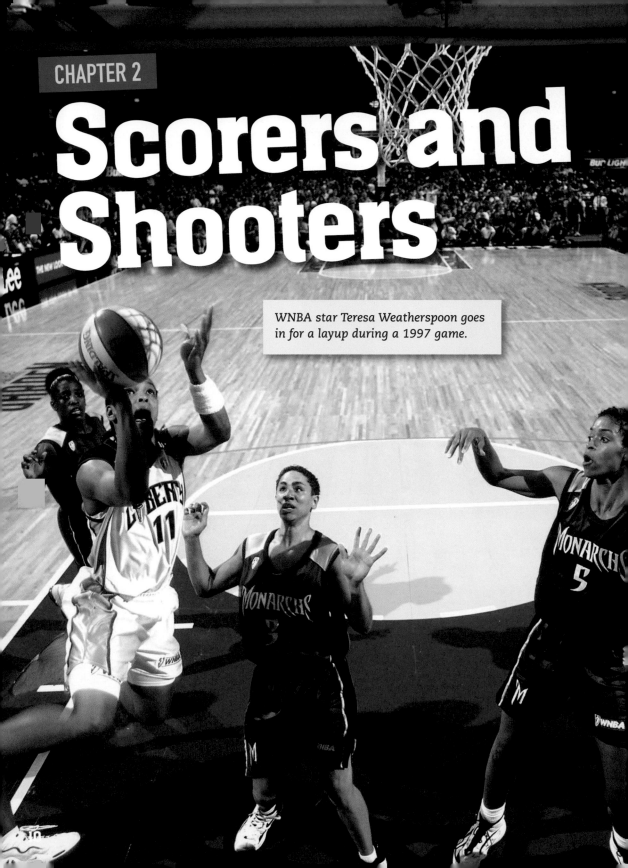

CHAPTER 2

Scorers and Shooters

WNBA star Teresa Weatherspoon goes in for a layup during a 1997 game.

Great scorers and shooters get nickname love too. Check out these players who rained threes and filled up the buckets.

TERESA "Spoon" WEATHERSPOON

New York Liberty point guard Teresa Weatherspoon played in the first season of the Women's National Basketball Association (WNBA) in 1997. Spoon, also known as T-Spoon, would hit one of the most amazing shots in WNBA history. It was a half-court **buzzer-beater** in the 1999 WNBA Finals.

JIMMY BUTLER: Jimmy Buckets

When Jimmy Butler was a teenager, his mother made him move out of her house. She did not like the way he was behaving. A friend's family took him in. But Butler knew he had to learn to work harder. The result is Jimmy Buckets. He's a player his team can count on to make a bucket when they need him to.

"Downtown" FREDDIE BROWN

Fred Brown hit shots from deep on the court. People said it seemed like he was shooting from downtown. In 1979, it was the first year the NBA allowed the 3-point shot. Brown made 44 percent of his shots. It was the best in the NBA.

The Splash Brothers high-five each other during a playoff game in 2019.

STEPH CURRY AND KLAY THOMPSON:
Splash Brothers

Some fans call a shot that swishes through the net a "splash." Steph Curry and Klay Thompson became Golden State Warriors teammates in 2011. Since then, fans have seen many splashes. Some say Curry and Thompson are the best shooters in the game today.

. . . .

LUKA DONČIĆ: El Matador

Luka Dončić is called El Matador. It means "The Bullfighter" in Spanish. Dončić played pro basketball in Spain as a teenager. This star guard hit the NBA with the Dallas Mavericks in 2018.

BALL IN THE FAMILY

Both Steph Curry and Klay Thompson come from athletic families. Both players' fathers, Dell Curry and Mychal Thompson, played pro basketball. Both players' mothers, Sonya Curry and Julie Thompson, played college volleyball. Both players have a brother (Seth Curry and Mychel Thompson) who made it to the NBA. Curry's sister, Sydel, was a college volleyball player. Thompson's brother, Trayce, made it to the major leagues in baseball.

> *Nancy Lieberman was known as Lady Magic later in her basketball career.*

NANCY LIEBERMAN: Lady Magic

Nancy Lieberman was an outstanding college and Olympic basketball player. At age 39, she also spent one season in the WNBA. She played her best basketball in the 1980s. That was at the same time as L.A. Lakers star Magic Johnson. His style of playing was a lot like Lieberman's.

GEORGE "The Iceman" GERVIN

George Gervin was just plain cool. Fans said the San Antonio Spurs star looked smooth. They also thought his game, with his special "finger roll" shot, was smooth and cool, like ice.

EARVIN "Magic" JOHNSON

When Earvin Johnson had the ball, he performed eye-popping plays. Magic got his nickname in high school. The hoops wizard never looked back. In his career, Johnson scored more than 17,000 points.

LARRY BIRD: Larry Legend

Larry Bird was one of the NBA's all-time great shooters. It's no wonder how he got his nickname. Larry **Legend** won three titles with the Boston Celtics in the 1980s. He was league **MVP** three times.

BEST OF THE REST: More Great Scorer and Shooter Nicknames

Jerry West: **Mr. Clutch**

Dwyane Wade: **Flash**

Jamaal Wilkes: **Silk**

Earl "**The Pearl**" Monroe

Shawn Kemp: **Reign Man**

Karl "**The Mailman**" Malone

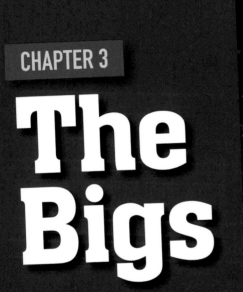

Besides Big Ticket, Kevin Garnett was also called KG.

CHAPTER 3

The Bigs

Most famous basketball players have been called big at some point. Big Ticket. Big Dog. Big Country. The list of nicknames is, well, big.

WILT CHAMBERLAIN:
The Big Dipper

Wilt Chamberlain was nicknamed The Big Dipper because he was so tall that he had to dip his head under doorframes. Wilt the Stilt—as he was also known—once scored 100 points in a game in 1962. It's a record that still stands.

KEVIN GARNETT:
Big Ticket

Kevin Garnett was just 19 years old when he made it to the NBA. He started with the Minnesota Timberwolves in 1995. Sportscaster Trent Tucker first called Garnett Big Ticket. People bought tickets to the games just to watch him play.

TIM DUNCAN:
The Big Fundamental

For 19 seasons, the San Antonio Spurs relied on center Tim Duncan for his skills. Duncan was nicknamed The Big **Fundamental** by another big man, center Shaquille O'Neal. O'Neal called him that because Duncan was good at passing, dribbling, shooting, and other fundamental skills.

OSCAR ROBERTSON:
The Big O

Oscar Robertson was the best do-it-all guard anyone had ever seen when he turned pro in 1960. The Big O could score, rebound, and pass. He won a championship with the Milwaukee Bucks in 1971.

Hoop Fact

Shaquille O'Neal had plenty of nicknames himself. They included The Big Aristotle, Big Fella, Shaq Fu, Shaq Daddy, and Diesel.

Shaquille O'Neal (#34) and Tim Duncan (#21) had many great battles in the 1990s and 2000s.

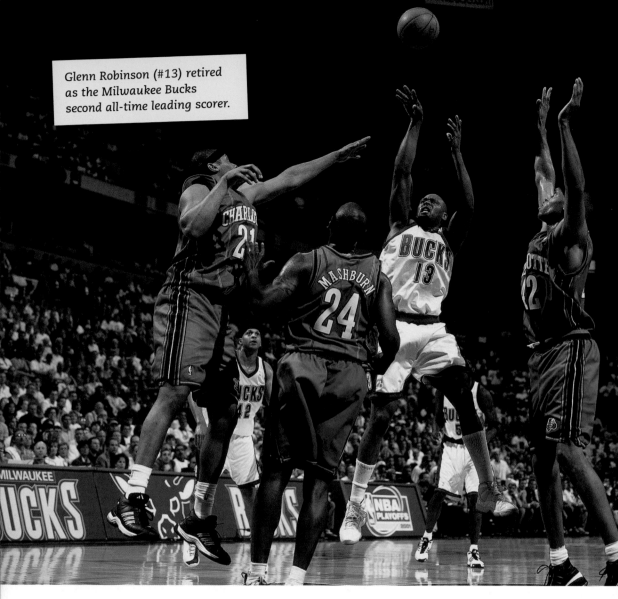

Glenn Robinson (#13) retired as the Milwaukee Bucks second all-time leading scorer.

GLENN "Big Dog" ROBINSON

Glenn Robinson got the nickname Big Dog for his tough style of play. The Purdue University star was the number-one overall pick of the 1994 NBA **Draft**. He went on to play for the Milwaukee Bucks.

BRYANT REEVES:
Big Country

Bryant Reeves looked like a farm boy from the country, and he was. When the big center took his first airplane trip in college, a teammate called him Big Country. Born in Oklahoma, Reeves played six years with the Vancouver Grizzlies.

Bryant "Big Country" Reeves (right) sometimes matched up against Patrick Ewing (#33). Ewing was called The Hoya Destroya in his college days. He played for the Georgetown University Hoyas.

BEST OF THE REST: Other Famous "Big" Nicknames

Sam Perkins: **Big Smooth**

Dave Cowens: **Big Red**

Elvin Hayes: **The Big E**

Ben Wallace: **Big Ben**

Steven Adams: **Big Kiwi**

Chauncey Billups: **Mr. Big Shot**

Robert Horry: **Big Shot Bob**

James Worthy: **Big Game James**

Damian Lillard: **Big Game Dame**

Cody Zeller: **The Big Handsome**

CHAPTER 4

The Littles

Long live the little guy! In a game full of long-legged leapers, these bite-sized b-ballers bounced their way to the top of the nickname game.

. . . .

CHRIS PAUL: **CP3**

Chris Paul's nickname uses his **initials** and his jersey number. Short and sweet, just like this speedy All-Star point guard.

Chris Paul led the NBA in steals per game in six different seasons.

NATE "Tiny" ARCHIBALD

Tiny Archibald was small, but his game was big. Archibald is the only player in NBA history to lead in both points and assists in a single season.

. . . .

TYRONE "Muggsy" BOGUES

Muggsy Bogues got his nickname during his childhood. A kid in his neighborhood said Bogues reminded him of a TV character named Muggsy. At 5-foot-3 (160 cm), Bogues was the shortest player to play in the NBA.

Muggsy Bogues played with the Toronto Raptors at the end of his career.

FRED "Curly" NEAL

Fred Neal was a longtime member of the Harlem Globetrotters. He was great at dribbling the ball. He also pulled off a lot of pranks on the court. The bald-headed point guard's nickname of Curly made perfect nonsense.

ANTHONY "Spud" WEBB

Spud Webb stood only 5-foot-7 (170 cm). It didn't stop him from winning the 1986 NBA Slam Dunk Contest. That's no small potatoes! Webb had a long NBA career. He played 13 seasons.

VINNIE "The Microwave" JOHNSON

Vinnie "The Microwave" Johnson wasn't the tallest player on the court. But the minute he came into the game, he started shooting. He could heat up quick and score in bunches. It earned him the nickname The Microwave.

"Pistol" PETE MARAVICH

"Pistol" Pete Maravich still holds the record for the highest points-per-game average in college basketball. He showed off his shooting skills for 10 seasons in the NBA. Maravich was so commonly called Pistol that he sometimes wore the nickname on the back of his game jersey.

Hoop Fact

Most Harlem Globetrotters had a nickname. Some of the best-nicknamed players included "Wee" Willie Gardner, Reece "Goose" Tatum, Meadowlark Lemon, and Nat "Sweetwater" Clifton.

"Curly" Neal (right) performs during a Harlem Globetrotters game.

BEST OF THE REST: Other Famous Point Guard Nicknames

Kenny "**The Jet**" Smith

Isiah Thomas: **Zeke**

Jason Williams: **White Chocolate**

Anfernee "**Penny**" Hardaway

Rafer Alston: **Skip to My Lou**

Craig "**Speedy**" Claxton

Eric "**Sleepy**" Floyd

Allen Iverson: **The Answer**

Lafayette "**Fat**" Lever

Gary Payton: **The Glove**

Jerome "**Pooh**" Richardson

Glenn "**Doc**" Rivers

It's easy to see why James Harden is called The Beard.

CHAPTER 5

The Wild and Weird

The easiest nicknames to remember are often the strangest. Some are funny. Some are a mouthful. Some are just weird.

JAMES HARDEN: The Beard

James Harden started growing his beard as a pro **rookie** in 2009. He hasn't shaved it off since. Who can argue with The Beard with stats and fame like his?

ANTHONY DAVIS: The Brow

Anthony Davis's nickname comes from a strange place. His eyebrows! The Brow's powerful blocks and soaring dunks make him a standout player.

CHARLES BARKLEY:
The Round Mound of Rebound

Nicknames that rhyme are fun. That's why Charles Barkley's The Round Mound of Rebound nickname sounds so good. Barkley took his rebounding and scoring worldwide. He led the U.S. Men's Olympic Basketball "Dream Team" in scoring in the 1992 Olympic Games.

KEVIN DURANT: Durantula

Kevin Durant has long, skinny arms and legs and is nearly 7 feet (213 cm) tall. It's easy to see why he was nicknamed after a spider. Many teams have felt the bite of a killer Durantula 3-pointer or dunk.

Hoop Fact

Many basketball teams have animal nicknames. Some players also have animal nicknames, such as Harry "The Horse" Gallatin, Earl "The Goat" Manigault, and Bill "The Owl Without a Vowel" Mlkvy.

Charles Barkley scores against Brazil during a 1992 Olympic Game.

GIANNIS ANTETOKOUNMPO:
The Alphabet

It's a mouthful to say Giannis Antetokounmpo's name. It has so many letters that some people call him The Alphabet. This superstar won the NBA's MVP award in 2019 and 2020.

JONQUEL JONES:
Bahamian Beast

WNBA center Jonquel Jones earned her nickname during a 2019 playoff game. Sportscaster Rebecca Lobo called Jones the Bahamian Beast for scoring 32 points and grabbing 18 rebounds. The Connecticut Sun player was born in the Bahamas.

NBA MVP Giannis Antetokounmpo was born in Athens, Greece.

DENNIS RODMAN:
Worm

Dennis Rodman wasn't always the tallest player under the basket. But he knew how to wriggle and twist to grab the ball. Rodman was nicknamed "Worm" for the way he would react while playing pinball as a kid. But the nickname also fit when Rodman became one the game's all-time best rebounders and defenders.

. . . .

The game of basketball is rich with nicknames. Only time will tell what new nicknames will bounce into basketball glory.

Dennis Rodman grabbed plenty of rebounds during his time with the Chicago Bulls.

BEST OF THE REST: Other Wild and Weird Nicknames

DeMarcus Cousins: **Boogie**

Stacey Augmon: **Plastic Man**

Bill Bradley: **Dollar Bill**

Brian Cardinal: **The Custodian**

"Never Nervous" Pervis Ellison

John Havlicek: **Hondo**

Fred Hoiberg: **The Mayor**

Tyler Hansbrough: **Psycho T**

Larry Johnson: **Grandmama**

Mark **"Mad Dog"** Madsen

GLOSSARY

buzzer-beater (BUZZ-ur-BEET-ur)—a shot scored just as the clock expires at the end of a period of play, especially one at the end of a game resulting in a win for the shooter's team

draft (DRAFT)—the process of choosing a person to join a sports team

fundamental (FUHN-duh-men-tuhl)—one of the basic and important parts of something

initial (UH-ni-shul)—the first letter of a name or word

legend (LEJ-uhnd)—a person among the best at what he or she does

MVP (EM-vee-pea)—an award that goes to the best player in a game or season; MVP stands for Most Valuable Player

record (REK-urd)—when something is done better than anyone has ever done it before

rookie (RUK-ee)—a first-year player

sportscaster (SPORTS-cast-ur)—someone who describes a sporting event

READ MORE

Moore, Madison. *More Than Just a Game: The Black Origins of Basketball.* Chicago: Albert Whitman & Company, 2021.

Slade, Suzanne. *Swish!: The Slam-Dunking, Alley-Ooping, High-Flying Harlem Globetrotters.* New York: Little, Brown and Company, 2020.

Storden, Thom. *Basketball's Greatest Buzzer-Beaters and Other Crunch-time Heroics.* North Mankato, MN: Capstone Press, 2020.

INTERNET SITES

NBA Players
nba.com/players

NBA & ABA Player Directory
basketball-reference.com/players/

Sports Illustrated Kids: Basketball
sikids.com/basketball

INDEX